THE WORLD OF C. P. SNOW

THE WORLD OF
C. P. SNOW

by

ROBERT GREACEN

with a Bibliography by

BERNARD STONE

SCORPION PRESS

First published in September 1962 by
Scorpion Press
Manor House, Pakefield Street, Lowestoft, Suffolk

Printed by Villiers Publications Ltd.,
Ingestre Road, London, N.W.5

List of Illustrations

THE WORLD OF C. P. SNOW

by Robert Greacen

English and American critics have, over the past five years or so, been increasingly convinced that in C. P. Snow we have a major talent in the novel. Few indeed, whatever their conclusion about Snow's stature as a novelist, would dare to take issue with these words of the English writer and scientist, William Cooper: ' C. P. Snow is a novelist of unique experience. At a period of history when the worlds of literature, and of science and technology, are sharply separated from each other, he has come to hold a key position in both simultaneously. A novelist by vocation, he is also a scientific administrator and man of affairs.'

The biographical facts about C. P. Snow may be stated quite simply. Born in relatively humble circumstances in Leicester in 1905 and educated locally, Charles Percy Snow began his career as a professional scientist, although he always had an ambition to become a creative writer. Winning a research scholarship to Cambridge University, he worked on molecular physics and became a Fellow of Christ's College in 1930. He remained in academic life until the outbreak of World War II, when he joined the Civil Service. As a scientist and a shrewd judge of human character he was principally concerned with the selection of scientific personnel. In the postwar years he has had further experience of these problems both in industry and as a Civil Service Commissioner.

Just before leaving Cambridge for the Civil Service in London, Snow started writing the ' Lewis Eliot ' sequence of novels, to be known on completion by the title of the first volume, *Strangers and Brothers* (1940). *The New Men* won the James Tait Black Memorial Prize — one of the leading British literary awards — for the best novel of 1954. *The Conscience of the Rich* was widely acclaimed in 1958, and *The*

9

Affair (1960) was a Book of the Month choice in the United States. For some years Snow has found time to act as an occasional book reviewer; he did a stint as a fiction critic for *The Sunday Times* and takes a keen interest in new writing in the U.S. as well as in England.

More important, perhaps, he has contributed articles dealing with the broad issues of our time to such journals as *The Observer* and *New Statesman*. Some of these ideas found expression in the Rede Lecture which he delivered at Cambridge in 1959 and which was published in that year by the Cambridge University Press. He has appeared on the Brains Trust panel of the B.B.C., a programme that is seen by several million viewers. His knighthood shows that his achievements in science, in the Civil Service, and in literature have been noted on the highest level. Recently he has been Visiting Professor of English at the University of California, Berkeley. In 1950 he married the distinguished novelist and literary critic, Pamela Hansford Johnson.

So much for the basic facts about this outward-looking, forceful, kindly personality who would give the stranger unaware of his achievements an immediate impression of human warmth combined with a quick, strong, but perhaps not obviously brilliant intelligence. Snow, who willingly accepts the description of scientific humanist, deprecates that dichotomy between the arts and science which can so oddly persist in a highly industrialised country like England (perhaps the situation has slightly changed for the better in the postwar years) and which ought to be actively discouraged by educationalists. Snow discussed this attitude in detail in his Rede Lecture, entitled *The Two Cultures and the Scientific Revolution*. In his own person he has bridged the gulf that is popularly supposed to exist between artist and scientist, between the man who feels and the man who does. His example (like the examples of those English writer-scientists, Dr. J. Bronowski and Alex Comfort) may well prove of great importance at a time when more and more stress is being laid on the need for first-class scientists and technologists, as exemplified by the founding of Churchill College, Cambridge.

Yet for Snow the scientific man is not the complete man: the stars mean astronomy *and* poetry. For him creative expression in literature is a necessity, not a luxury or sideline interest. To risk a generalisation: the single theme that exercises Snow's mind in creative writing is ambition and the struggle for power among men. What he seeks to examine closely are the moral problems and dilemmas which ambitious men must constantly face. Snow's Lewis Eliot, the narrator of the ' Strangers and Brothers ' series, reflects in *Homecomings* (one of the three best novels in the series):

> When I was a young man, too poor to give much thought to anything but getting out of poverty, I had dreamed of great success at the Bar; since then I had kept an interest in success and power which was, to many of my friends, forbiddingly intense. And, of course, they were not wrong: if a man spends half of his time discussing basketball, thinking of basketball, examining with passionate curiosity the intricacies of basketball, it is not unreasonable to suspect him of a somewhat excessive interest in the subject . . . Sheila had ignored my liking for power, while Margaret actively detested it. . . . Now that I felt a theme in my life closing, I thought it likely that I had started off with an interest in power greater than that of most reflective men, but not a tenth of Lufkin's or Rose's, nothing like enough to last me for a lifetime. I expected that I should keep an eye open for the manoeuvres of others: who will get the job? and why? and how? I expected also that sometimes, as I watched others installed in jobs I might once have liked, I should feel regret. That did not matter much. Beneath it all, a preoccupation was over.

In this passage Lewis Eliot reveals that his passionate interest in success and power has somewhat diminished. Later, in the same book, we find that Eliot, distressed by the result of an interview in which his old friend George Passant fails to get a permanent job in the Civil Service, turns against the men who wield power:

> It had come pretty easy, it had not given me much regret, to slip out of the struggles of power — as a rule I did not mind seeing the places of power filled by the Osbaldistons, those who wanted them more. But that morning, gazing blankly down at the

11

sunny street, I was wretched because I was not occupying them myself. Then and only then could I have done something for George and those like him. The men I sat with in their offices, with their moral certainties, their comfortable, conforming indignation which never made them put a foot out of step — they were the men who managed the world, they were the people who in any society came out on top. They had virtues denied the rest of us: I had to give them my respect. But that morning I was on the other side.

Here we find that Lewis Eliot has come to value power only in so far as it would enable him to help those who need and desire assistance; and this would seem to reflect Snow's own point of view.

Another interesting point arises. Can a feeling of personal inadequacy — or, strangely enough, even diffidence — sometimes lie behind the urge for dominance? One thinks of Paul Jago in *The Masters* (1951). Or can a man achieve real power solely by good means? What will he do with the power once he gets it? These questions all crop up in the ' Lewis Eliot ' sequence. Eliot, the narrator, is not perhaps of primary importance; his own life matters less than the fact that he is in a position to take us behind the scenes in various professions — the law, Civil Service, the life of Cambridge dons — and to describe accurately and reflect on the doings of others. Naturally, there is an element of Snow in Eliot — they are of an age and share a common background — but of course he is not Snow. Eliot is used in the counterpointing of ' direct experience ' and ' observed experience ', to use Snow's own words. This counterpointing is indeed, in the opinion of Norman Podhoretz, the American critic, ' the main principle governing the organisation of the whole series.'

The theme of Snow's concern with men attempting self-fulfilment through power, and the self-knowledge and responsibility power sometimes brings, may be found at its purest and most intense in *The Masters*. The old Master of a Cambridge college is dying. Soon his thirteen colleagues will elect a successor: will it be Paul Jago, a warmly human, moody man of Anglo-Irish origin and a man inclined to emotional extra-

12

vagrance, or the solidly based Crawford, talented, shrewd, reliable, but a trifle unimaginative? Jago is on the arts side, though his academic achievement has not been distinguished: Crawford, the scientist, has a considerable reputation outside Cambridge and is a Fellow of the Royal Society. Factions arise, and strong emotions come to the surface and occasionally explode.

Here then in small compass we may see the whole business of practical politics. If it is not pretty, it is certainly not disgusting: it happens every day at all levels, whether in small-town administration, in Westminster, Washington, or Moscow. Given a short briefing, Khrushchev could understand what *The Masters* is all about. Most critics agree that this is Snow's most successful novel so far. Certainly it achieves artistic unity more surely than the others. Here and there in it Snow's style, for the most part serviceable rather than memorable or individual, is heightened into something near to poetic statement. More than in his other novels we can see what Helen Gardner is getting at when she says that in Snow's work ' the ultimate quest is not for success, but for value and meaning.'

One last point about this work is that it reveals a surprising tenderness towards and understanding of women. This ability of Snow's has been observed by Derek Stanford:

> It might not be thought that Snow — with his ' masculine' interests in science and politics — should prove himself, as a novelist, so excellent a portrayer of women. One has only to turn to Sheila (Lewis Eliot's first wife) and compare her with Roy Calvert to notice the superior way in which the author has handled her. Both these characters are studies in mental alienation, both ' cases' proving, in the long run, fatal. But whereas Sheila's psychological illness is traced with clear attentiveness from the start, that of Calvert is obfuscated by certain intellectual interpolations.

The Conscience of the Rich (1958) is also concerned with power — and its renunciation. Its very title furnishes a clue to content. At the beginning the reader is taken back to Lewis Eliot's early days in London in the 1930's when he had just

13

qualified as a barrister. Through Charles March, a young man whom he has come across as a law student and very much liked, Eliot meets a wealthy family for the first time. They are Jews who have money and an assured social position. We go with the young provincial lawyer into the houses of the great and are induced to share Eliot's thrill at making his way into the alien but nevertheless acceptable world of the rich. The Jewish Marches, with their banking connections, live in a comfortable way that Eliot as yet knows little about. Yet young March, over-aware of his Jewish separateness, considers himself unfortunate and is driven to say to Eliot: ' Since I was a child I haven't been allowed to forget that other people see me through different eyes.' He goes on: ' They label me with a difference I can't accept.' Snow gives an utterly convincing and valid picture of Anglo-Jewry; he can understand and sympathise with the sense of insecurity with which every Jew is born, even in a country so tolerant of minorities as England.

Old Mr. March — ' Mr. L.' to his children — is a delightful character study. A fundamentally good man, he behaves badly towards his son Charles for refusing to be a March. Charles can find himself only by renouncing the life of a rich man's son and becoming a doctor instead of a gentleman banker or successful barrister, helped on by using the family connections. All the time in reading this novel one is aware of the action's taking place in the 1930's, that period of left-wing agitation. *The Conscience of the Rich*, therefore, takes one a long way both in time and setting from *Strangers and Brothers* (1940), which is set in a provincial town not unlike Snow's home town of Leicester, and which introduces that strange but compelling person, George Passant, who also appears in later volumes.

Snow's deepest exploration of personal unhappiness will be found in *Homecomings* (1956), the novel which moved so stern an academic critic as Helen Gardner and convinced her that her earlier and harsh judgment of Snow had been ill-considered. As she put is: ' C. P. Snow is attempting something which, on this scale, has no parallel in English, a panoramic novel which accepts fully the limitations of narration in the first person.'

Other nations frequently borrow the English phrase for a specifically English concept — ' le fair play ', as the French say. This notion of fair dealing, indeed of simple justice being done and being *seen* to be done, is central to Snow's latest novel, *The Affair* (1960), a fine addition to the sequence. In it, Snow examines the actions and motives of the Fellows of a fictional Cambridge college as they sit in judgment on a young Fellow named Howard, who has been accused of a scientific fraud. The year is 1953, just seventeen years after the election of Crawford, the scientist, as Master of the college in *The Masters*. Nobody likes Howard, a surly loutish young man who happens to have extreme left-wing views and has not just a chip on his shoulder but a log. Howard has been deprived of his Fellowship after an investigation, and the matter is being kept secret. Nobody wants news of it to leak into the papers. Not one of the twenty Fellows, whatever his political attitude, doubts for a moment that the man is guilty. Great care has been taken to ensure that the college ' trial ' of Howard by the Court of Seniors is conducted with even more scrupulous fairness than an ordinary process at law.

Then, suddenly, doubt springs up in circumstances somewhat resembling those of the Dreyfus affair. Is the detestable Howard really guilty? It is the notorious French ' affair ' which gives its title to this novel; Snow explains in a prefatory note that years ago, when he started thinking of the theme of justice, the Dreyfus case was his starting point. The scientific fraud was suggested by what the author terms ' the picturesque case of Rupp.' The Fellows split into two parties, one of which is set on having justice done. On the surface it might seem a plain matter of good versus evil, of decency against blind prejudice; but that would be a false oversimplification. Human affairs are more complex than that. Snow is at pains to show how even the noblest of men have mixed motives. Some on the ' wrong 'side — like Arthur Brown, the ' worthy Brown ' as Winslow scathingly calls him — are far more compassionate than others (such as Skeffington) who champion the unhappy young scientist.

Skeffington, brave and honourable, decides on justice at whatever cost to his own reputation or anyone else's. Yet Snow notes that ' inside that feeling, there was no kindness towards Howard. There was no trace of brotherly emotion at all. The only residue of feeling he had for Howard was contempt.' (The idea of brotherliness is important to Snow: he speaks in *Homecomings* of George Passant's being a ' human brother ', and he closely examines Lewis Eliot's relationship with his own real brother. One must also bear in mind the title of the entire series and of the first volume in it, *Strangers and Brothers*.) Thus, Snow argues, self-centred men can sacrifice their own interests for the sake of a cold, abstract justice, while warm-hearted men may find plausible reasons for resisting it. This paradox lies at the heart of *The Affair*.

Anyone who delighted in *The Masters* will be interested to know what has happened to the old college hands in the intervening seventeen years. By the time *The Affair* is taking place, ten new Fellows have come on the scene, and these Lewis knows only slightly. At one point he thinks: ' True, some of those I had known best, were dead,' and in his mind he calls — Proust-like — the sad roll: Despard-Smith, dead, Eustace Pilbrow, dead, Chrystal, dead, Roy Calvert, dead. Still, the genial and rubicund Arthur Brown goes on quietly managing college business, and giving his little wine-sipping parties. Long ago he came to terms — practical man that he is — with Crawford, the Master, a man he has never fundamentally liked and whom he opposed seventeen years earlier in the contest for the Mastership. Brown's candidate then was Jago.

All through *The Affair* we are kept aware of the changes, especially the social changes, that have occurred since the middle-thirties; and Snow appears to enjoy the role of social historian. There are, for instance, no servants going round now carrying trays covered with green baize; and the young Fellows actually discuss college business with their wives. Throughout the novel we are conscious, too, of the next

16

C. P. Snow

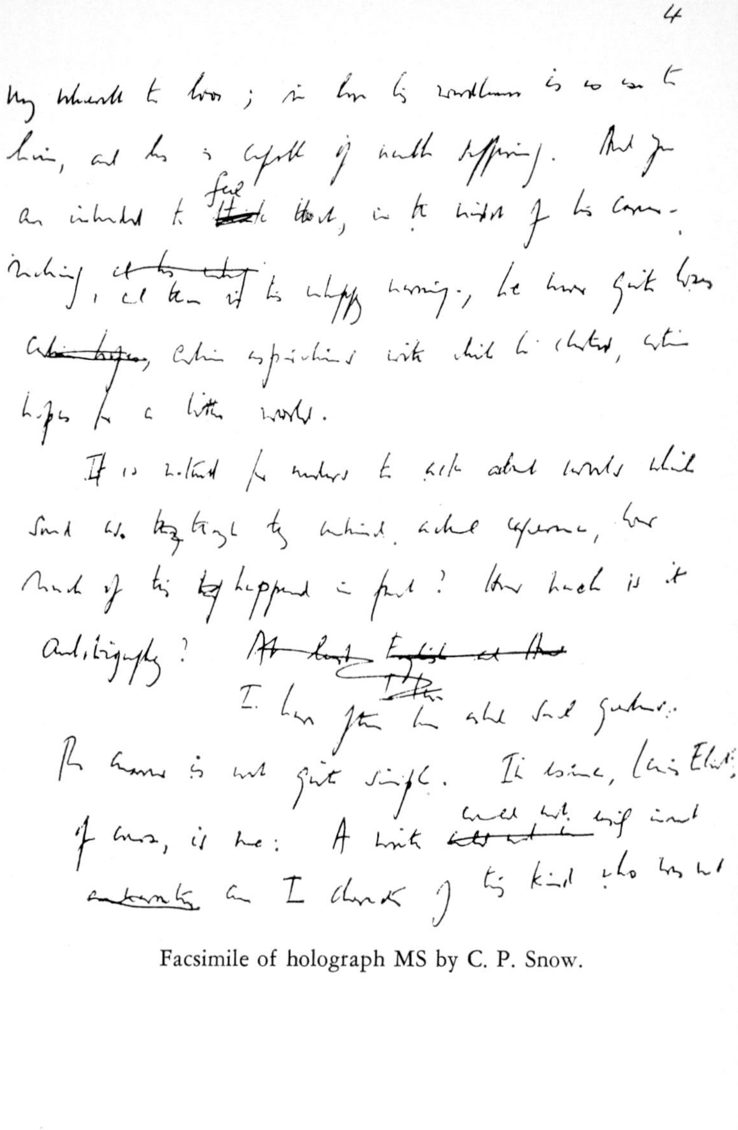

Facsimile of holograph MS by C. P. Snow.

election for the Mastership, due in about six months' time, when Crawford leaves the Master's Lodge. The two most likely candidates are Arthur Brown and the scientist, Getliffe, now the famous *Sir* Francis Getliffe. We keep wondering how their behaviour in the Howard ' affair ' will affect their chances.

The Affair is one of the strongest links in the chain of novels. It fits admirably into the broad design, as well as being in itself an intriguing narrative. And if the implications of the Howard case are peculiarly English, the middle-of-the-road solution could hardly have been worked out in any other country. As Derek Stanford says:

> Within the Lewis Eliot sequence, I would place *The Affair* very near the top. It lacks the artistic roundness of that world-within-a-world which we find in *The Masters,* and it has not quite the gravelling pathos of that domestic narrative of misfortune, *Homecomings.* But if it lacks the finish and unity of the first and the deep disturbing pull on our heartstrings of the second, it is richly artistic in its own way. The double split within the college in *The Affair* — as to Howard's guilt or innocence, and as to the coming magisterial election — makes for subtle cross-currents in character-reaction.

In his Rede Lecture Snow boldly declares at the outset: ' By training I was a scientist: by vocation I was a writer.' For thirty years Snow has mixed with both scientists and writers. An obvious proof of this combination of interests is that exciting novel of his, *The New Men* (1954), at the core of which is an event important not only in science but in human destiny, the discovery of atomic fission. He tells us in the Rede Lecture how there have been many days when he spent the working hours with scientists before going off to pass the evening with literary friends. ' Constantly,' he writes, ' I felt I was moving among two groups — comparable in intelligence, identical in race, not grossly different in social origin, earning about the same incomes, who had almost ceased to communicate at all, who in intellectual, moral and psychological climate had so little in common that instead of going from Burlington House or South Kensington to Chelsea, one might have crossed an ocean.' How is it that the chemists and physicists and engineers have ceased to speak to the poets and critics and novelists? Writers seem only to speak to a handful of scientists. Is it a bad thing and can anything be done about it? These are the questions to which Snow has attempted a number of answers.

That this polarisation — seen in an extreme form in England but applicable also to Western Europe and the United States — is a loss to the community at large Snow rightly has no doubt. We lose both personally and as a society. This predicament has come about principally because of our English educational system, in which children begin to specialise at an earlier age than in the United States or even in the Soviet Union; and Snow appears to lay the fault at the door of the Oxford and Cambridge method of awarding scholarships. It can be argued of course that children ought not, as in most Continental countries, to be burdened with too many subjects. If they are, they will have less time for ' character-building ' activities — games, clubs, and so on — and some of the subjects may indeed be studied rather superficially. Even allowing for these arguments Snow builds up a powerful case to show that the present rigidity of English education means that the country is not adequately coping with the scientific revolution in which we are living. He maintains, and gives figures to prove his contention, that other countries are doing better. He emphasises that England educates far fewer scientists proportionately than do the Americans or the Russians. It is just possible that Snow's Rede Lecture may have a very considerable effect on English educational policy.

Snow occasionally writes on matters of international interest, although he does not seem to take any very clearly defined political line. Nevertheless, it would be true to say that politically he is a bit left of centre; and this point of view may be glimpsed in his fiction, although he is far from being a partisan. (He sometimes puts up a better case for men who might be considered political enemies than for those who are on his own side, as if he were saying that sometimes Conservatives are good men personally, while ' progressives ' may well be self-centred and opportunist.) One of Snow's most cogent statements appeared in an article in the *Observer* in July 1958 under the title ' Man in Society '. Snow began by insisting on the paradox that the Western society responsible for the horrors of Auschwitz and the catastrophe of Hiroshima has in recent years shown more tolerance and consideration for the weak and unfortunate than have ever been shown by any other large society in human history. He pointed out how some of the intellectual and moral giants — Einstein and Niels Bohr, for instance — played an important part in the development of the atom bomb. There it is: man has an infinite capacity for self-transcending conduct on the one hand and for utter beastliness on the other.

But that is not all:

> In each of our individual lives there is, of course, something beyond human help. Each of us has to live part of his life alone: and he has to die alone. That part of our experience is right outside time and history, and progress has no meaning there. In this sense, the individual condition is tragic. But that is no excuse for not doing our best with the social condition.

Snow goes on to characterise the refuge in despair of certain intellectuals as treacherous and shoddy, asserting that there is no contracting-out of the human condition, no funk-hole anywhere, no getting away from ourselves.

In the same article Snow stresses the point that although from time to time some of us affect to despise the idea of ' progress ' as an outdated Victorian idea, we have indeed progressed. He feels that we have no right to tell the Asians (millions of whom have not enough food to eat) that progress is bunk. He can find hope in the fact that despite the shadows cast by bombs and concentration camps we have not become so dehumanised that we no longer get ' morally concerned about the fate of one murderer or cross because a lonely and impoverished old man doesn't have enough calls from the District Visitor.' Snow thinks that as long as man exists — and he reminds us that man is the toughest of all species, as the quick recovery of the appallingly war-devastated areas helps to prove — despite all his limitations he will from time to time ' stretch a little beyond himself.'

As a practical thinker, Snow's message appears to be simply this: it is hard at the moment to see the way ahead, and there will surely be a lot of difficulties and even horrors in front of us, but we must not give up. Difficulties, given intelligence and good-will, can be overcome. Science is here to help man, not to destroy him; and science is on the side of optimism. He believes we have several good scientific reasons for taking the long-term view that humanity is indestructible. That is what Snow is saying, in both his fiction and non-fiction, to one reader at least. The world of C. P. Snow has its tragic undertones, to be sure, but its creator believes that in the end humanity will come out on the side of reason and kindness; and that when some of the contemporary tensions can be eased, the strangers and enemies of today may well become the brothers and friends of tomorrow.

Little or nothing has been said so far about the first six of Snow's novels. Three are outside the Lewis Eliot sequence: *Death under Sail* (1932), *New Lives for Old* (1933) and *The Search* (1934). The other three, which belong to the Eliot series comprise the novel which gives its name to the entire work, *Strangers and Brothers* (1940), *The Light and the Dark* (1947) and *Time of Hope* (1949). It will be noticed in passing that there was a gap of seven years (1940-7) in Snow's novel writing, to be accounted for by the fact that their author was working at full pressure in the Civil Service.

These six novels have not been examined until now since they did not fit naturally into the general survey of Snow already attempted and in which some comment has been made on the more artistically successful later novels. Yet, for all that, as we shall see, the early novels led quite naturally to achievements on a bigger scale like *The Masters*.

Snow's literary beginnings were relatively unambitious. His first novel, *Death under Sail*, is the story of a murder on a sailing boat on the Norfolk Broads. It is ' ordinary ' in the sense that it fits neatly into the time-honoured pattern of detective fiction. And yet, perhaps, as William Cooper says: ' The plot grows out of the characters rather than the characters out of the plot.'

People have always fascinated Snow; he likes them, which is more than can be said for some of our *angst*-mongers. He is for life and against death. Looking at *Death under Sail* now, in the light of Snow's later books, one gets a foretaste of the accomplished older novelist in the young scientist who wrote the book as a relief from his hard scientific grind. Snow reveals in it something of the high spirits that might not have been expected in a scholarship boy who had made his own way to a Fellowship of Christ's, Cambridge. William Cooper aptly remarks that *Death under Sail* was ' an odd but nevertheless remarkable beginning '.

In 1933 *New Lives for Old* was published anonymously. The theme is the discovery of a hormone that could be of use in the rejuvenation process. Snow looks with a Wellsian outlook into the future — the narrative is spread over the 1950-80 period approximately. Most people might think that Snow would show the consequences of the discovery as a great boon to mankind. On the contrary, he sees in the ultimate consequences a moral and economic deterioration. Science — or at least scientific discoveries — are not necessarily on the side of the human race. Anonymity of publication was due to the fact that Snow, a fast-rising research scientist, feared that publication of the novel under his own name would have stimulated professional envy.

It was possible to publish *Death under Sail* under his own name since the writing and reading of detective novels are generally accepted as relaxation for the busy professional man (nobody thinks less well of Cecil Day Lewis as a poet and critic because he is also ' Nicholas Blake ', or of the scholar J. I. M. Stewart because he is ' Michael Innes ').

New Lives for Old showed that a new and significant storyteller was in the making; and that its author would not take the merely facile view that all that happened in the scientific

21

world was obviously for the best. Human beings, with all their instinctual drives and their contradictoriness, also mattered. Here was a writer who increasingly asked why people behaved in the irrational way they so often do. The answers were to come later.

Having launched himself as a writer outside the scientific field — and at this point it may be mentioned that the reader with a background in physics may wish to refer to Snow's contributions to the Proceedings of the Royal Society 1928-9, 1930-2, 1935, to which he contributed papers on Molecular Structure—C. P. Snow produced *The Search* (1934), the novel into which he poured all his earlier experiences. He wrote a note to the effect ' this is a work of fiction, not a concealed autobiography. The ' I ' of the story is not myself; his experiences are not mine nor are the characters who enter into them meant to be people I have met in life.' And yet this narrative of the struggles, disappointments and successes of a young scientist, Arthur Miles, told straightforwardly in the first person, must surely have been partially based on the experiences of the author and his friends. Such telling details, related with the zest of a still young man, is not to be conjured up out of the air. Yet naturally we must be on our guard against reading into every incident a parallel happening in Snow's own life. The true novelist invents.

Miles makes his way by means of scholarships (harder to win in the 1920's than now) from lower middle-class origins to a position of some power in his chosen field. The conflict in *The Search* is simply between the pursuit of scientific truth on the one hand and career-building on the other. Can these be reconciled? Must there be a clash? Miles, having done great things in research, finds himself involved in the behind-the-scenes affairs of a proposed research institute; and because of this involvement he makes a mistake in his own research work that adversely affects his reputation. Thus he is thrown back on himself and has to examine his conscience in an attempt to know precisely what kind of man he is. If, as Snow reminds us from time to time, a man dies alone, then also for much of his life he has to live with himself, with his own past and present, and the consequences of his own actions. Thus it is with Arthur Miles.

In the very first chapter of *The Search* we see how science opens up for Miles as a child. He goes for a walk with his father one Sunday evening in a provincial town and they look up at the stars.

> I was happily excited. The night had taken hold of me. I wanted to do something with those stars. I did not quite know what, but I was elated. Their beauty stirred me, but it was not only that. If I had been older, I should have said I wanted to know, to understand, to alter. I wanted to rush out and have them for my own. I laughed ' I'm going to find out all about them.'

A child's decision can affect the whole course of a life. Some of us will recall the excitement of discovering poetry and the determination that we should write poetry ourselves. Similarly, young Arthur Miles' mind is set alight by the making of a telescope, fussing about with tubes and lenses. On another occasion he is fascinated by the excitement of his science master when he decides one day to cut out the usual drill of setting the boys to heat pieces of wood and mess about with ' combustion-tubes ' and, instead, talk to them about the great new stride forward in atomic physics : ' If you split up an atom of lead, you'd get — pieces of positive and negative electricity. Just that. Just positive and negative electricity. That's all matter is.'

Miles is followed through his school and university (King's College, London, and Cambridge) career. We are told about his friendships — Sheriff, a fellow scientist, and Hunt, a bright young economist who disappointingly gets lost in provincial schoolmastering. Too hard a worker and too shy to be a womaniser Miles' principal affair and the events leading up to his marriage reveal his emotional relationships with women. There is a contrast in technical ability between Miles and Sheriff. Whereas Miles bubbles over with scientific ideas, Sheriff is relatively short on initiative but possesses ' the most delicate — what shall I call it? — manual imagination that I had ever seen.'

More scientific terminology comes into *The Search* than into any of the later novels — more, perhaps, than even in *The New Men,* which is concerned with nuclear fission — but in a fairly long novel the reader can take it. Early on in his research career Miles has been exploring the possibilities of crystallography :

> To begin with I was going to start on a safe problem. . . . So I decided to work immediately on the structure of some of the manganates; the arrangement of the atoms seemed to me almost certain to fall into one of the simpler symmetries, and yet, for some reason, they were still unknown.

He also brings out as forcibly as anywhere else the excitement for a young man of the great discoveries in the Cavendish Laboratory in Cambridge. Thus, sitting in a crowded lecture room, he had a preview of the news that even the Royal Society and the world in general would not know for another month or two. And all the time, in the Cambridge streets, Miles could see if not speak to his heroes : Rutherford, the Danish Niels Bohr, the Russian Kapitza, Dirac (' of whom I heard it prophesied very early that he would be another Newton ') and Eddington. Good was it in that atomic dawn to be young and brilliant and in Cambridge.

The Search, then, takes us through a picture gallery of scientists. If it is less skilfully written than some of the novels Snow was to write later, it makes up for a certain diffuseness by its energy and enthusiasm. Had the reviewers of 1934 been more astute they would have hailed *The Search* as a novel far outside the usual run-of-the-mill fiction. They did not realise that a writer had emerged whose work opened up a completely new vein. The fault may not have been wholly in the critics themselves but in their arts-and-classics background that left, and unfortunately still leaves, Englishmen of education unaware of the role of the pure and applied scientists in our divided culture. As we approach the Common Market, and grapple with the realities of boosting production and exports, the work

Dust-jacket designed by Sidney Nolan for the first English
edition of *The Affair*.

Sir Charles Snow, accompanied by the Principal of St. Andrews University, Sir Malcolm Knok, leaving the Collegiate Chapel of St. Salvator's on the occasion of his installation as Rector, April 13th, 1962.

of a C. P. Snow has an increasing relevance 'for us all.

Now we must return to the Lewis Eliot sequence and look at the first three volumes. The title-volume, *Strangers and Brothers,* which came out during the first year of the war, covers the period 1925-33. The principal character in it is George Passant, a solicitor's clerk in his middle twenties, working in the offices of the leading firm in Lewis Eliot's home town in the midlands. To supplement his meagre income he gives law lectures at the local technical institute. Thus he comes into contact with a number of young people just embarking on their careers; and they look up to the articulate, unconventional, sensual-natured, idealistic George Passant not only for help in their studies but with their personal lives as well. These provincial young men live through the 1920's in an atmosphere of keenness for acquiring knowledge and skills. Passant, their father-figure, advises and encourages. Snow sees him as a man of basic integrity and great intelligence who might well have a dazzling future.

And yet. . . . What is the weakness in Passant's nature? Perhaps it may be found in a too open sensuality, one that is not masked by discretion. At the end of the narrative of *Strangers and Brothers* Passant just manages to escape from a charge of criminal and somewhat petty fraud. Jack Cotery, one of Passant's group, nearly brings about the disgrace of a man who seems far above anything mean or squalid.

Snow seems to have given a lot of sympathy as well as gone to enormous pains to establish the duality in Passant's character; and of course Passant memorably crops up again in *Homecomings,* in a setting far removed from the provincial town of Eliot's youth and the lower middle-class people with whom they then almost exclusively mixed. *Strangers and Brothers* may not be the most artistically satisfying in the series but it is indispensable to anyone who wishes to savour the strangely compelling personality of George Passant. Meeting Passant, even in fiction, is a rewarding experience. Too weak to become a great man he, for all that, possesses some of the elements of greatness.

While it would be wrong to suppose that *Strangers and Brothers* is a one-character novel, the young people in it are somewhat shadowy. George Passant holds them together by his dynamism; and his weekend parties at a farmhouse just outside the town further their intellectual and, one gathers, sexual experience. He helps them to work out their adult personalities.

Time of Hope (1949) starts in 1914 with Lewis Eliot a child of nine; and, written around Eliot's own life-experience as a first-person narrative, we are taken up to 1933, the year George Passant finds himself in trouble. Now just as Passant had a flaw in his nature, so has Lewis Eliot. One does not need to be steeped in Freudianism to notice the direct cause in the mother-son relationship, one that is just faintly reminiscent of that in another midland novel, Lawrence's *Sons and Lovers*. Eliot's mother is both dominating and loving, and keen that he should succeed in life. The boy cannot fully respond to her love. He tries to cope by being absent-minded, ' distant ', evasive. This pattern is repeated in his relationships with other women. Quite simply he reacts as best he can against feminine possessiveness.

Eliot begins as a clerk in the local government service but works in his spare time for the Bar. (One is always staggered by the capacity for both work and purposive relaxation in Snow's heroes — a full-time job and hard study on the side do not prevent them from having an exciting social and artistic life. The answer may be that they are expert in organising their time.) Eliot makes friends and by the age of twenty-eight has qualified as a barrister. Judged by provincial, or indeed any, standards, he has done better for himself than might have been expected. In his own eyes his career does not come up to his former hopes. What has gone wrong?

Since he was twenty Eliot has been in love with a beautiful girl called Sheila Knight, the daughter of a shrewd, self-centred and hypocritical clergyman. The girl's mother, coarse, vulgar and moneyed, is devoted to her husband and caters for his every whim. Sheila herself, not surprisingly, has no capacity for love. She has a compulsion to turn in savage resentment on anyone who reveals his fondness for her. Lewis marries her knowing that she does not love him; he knows that she can neither give nor take affection, and this limitation of hers actually appeals to him. *Time of Hope,* like *The Search,* deals with a provincial young man fighting for his room at the top; but the more important aspect of it is the exploration of the man-woman relationship. Lewis painfully acquires self-awareness, although it will be some years before he finally shakes himself free of Sheila and the need to bestow pity rather than to experience love. That day of fulfilment does come and the key to it will be found towards the end of *Homecomings* (1956) when, with his second wife Margaret, Eliot loses his sense of foreboding:

> We were in sight of home. A light was shining in one room: the others stood black, eyeless, in the leaden light. It was a home-coming such as, for years, I thought I was not to know. Often in my childhood, I had felt dread as I came near home. It had been worse when I went, as a young man, towards the Chelsea house. Now, walking with Margaret, that dread had gone. In sight of home my steps began to quicken, I should soon be there with her.
>
> It was a homecoming such as I had imagined when I was lonely, but as one happening to others, not to me.

Eliot has at last managed to reach out to another human being in a way that some people nowadays only achieve after years of psychiatric help.

In *The Light and the Dark* (1947) the reader will find an extended study of Roy Calvert, a cousin of Lewis Eliot's first wife Sheila. Calvert came into *Strangers and Brothers* as a boy, but by this time — the period covered runs from 1935 to 1943 — is a graduate of Snow's fictional Cambridge college. By 1935 Lewis Eliot has been elected to his Fellowship. An orientalist, Calvert is beginning to win a reputation for decyphering ancient texts; he has an easy command of various modern languages. Good-looking, rich, witty, *sympathique,* Calvert finds an entrée into the homes of distinguished men and into the hearts of women. The Master of the college takes him up and the Master's daughter takes him into her heart if not her bed. The stiff-lipped Master's wife, Lady Muriel, accepts him socially.

Yet for all his gifts and attainments Roy Calvert is profoundly unhappy. His problem, it is hinted, is manic depression. Put in a different way he is ' unhappily in love with God ', yet somehow unable to believe in God's very existence or love for mankind. One night Calvert, in a manic outburst, tells Lewis Eliot ' I hate the stars ', as if to say that he hates the mystery of life. One never quite knows what factors in Calvert's heredity or upbringing account for his illness — and indeed it is an illness of an intensity that should properly be treated by a psychiatrist. Snow leaves the matter deliberately vague, possibly to heighten the ' romantic ' element in Calvert's make-up.

Rumour has it that Calvert indulges privately in a wild life of alcohol and mistresses, although he keeps it carefully hidden from the college; and for once the suspicions of the staid, respectable Fellows are justified. Lewis Eliot finds in himself a deep understanding, even a profound pity, for Calvert. He realises why Calvert chooses to work on texts dealing with the Manichaen heresy, one in which man's spirit was supposed to belong to the *light* and his body to the *dark*. Hence the division and conflict in Calvert's own nature that lead to dissipation and unhappiness. Cycles of sparkling self-confidence alternate with others of blackness and futility.

Each time Calvert gets in the grip of a profound depression he can only find release in some action that is bitter and destructive. Then he becomes calm again; but his wild act lives on in the minds of his colleagues, and in a closed society like a Cambridge college it is not quickly forgotten or forgiven. Since the period is the 1930's Calvert finds himself attracted to the Nazis on his frequent visits to Germany, no doubt since he has a yearning for obedience to authority. If he cannot prostrate himself before God he will at least bow the knee in the direction of Nordic man. But he does not become so deeply involved with Nazism that he wants to defy his own country on the outbreak of war. He deliberately leaves a safe job and becomes a bomber pilot largely because he wishes to have as dangerous a war as possible. We learn of Calvert's death in

Homecomings and Eliot's reaction to it is worth quoting.

> Then, one morning in May, I heard of Roy Calvert's death. He had been my closest friend: though my friendships with George Passant and Charles March and my brother had been strong, this was different in kind. I had come to know him when I was most distracted about Sheila; he had seemed the most fortunate of men, he had given me sympathy more penetrating than anyone else's, but he too was afflicted, with a melancholy that in the end made his life worthless. I had tried to support him; for a while, perhaps, I was some use, but not for long. Now he was dead, and I could not get away from my sadness. It stayed like smoked glass between me and the faces in the streets.

The Light and the Dark is a darkly romantic book, a novel about an absurdly attractive yet inescapably doomed man; a man who, loved by the gods, is marked down for early destruction. It helps to answer the criticism that Snow can only deal effectively with the Sir Hector Roses and Lufkins, men who walk ' the corridors of power ', if that criticism were not answered by the tenderness and understanding he shows to women characters like Sheila Knight. A more telling adverse comment may be that Snow has left too many gaps in our knowledge of Calvert's motivation. For all that, the reader is willing to accept Calvert as a real and credible human being, though of a kind rarely to be encountered.

The entire Lewis Eliot sequence interlocks at point after point, although the reader curious for a first taste of this *roman fleuve* can pick up any one book at random and enjoy it. The novels do not need to be read either in the order in which they were published or according to the period covered in each volume. Yet one does well to keep in mind as many as possible of the characters who appear, vanish for a time and appear yet again: Passant, Calvert, Arthur Brown, the Marches, the Knights. Not for nothing has the series been given the general title of *Strangers and Brothers,* for Snow frequently makes a similar point in his non-fiction. He asserts the brotherhood of man; all men are human, even though some — like Passant and Calvert — are more human than others. Then there is the stark fact of human isolation, inescapable even for the most extravert of men. Each man has these two sides to his nature. The duality fascinates Snow; and perhaps because it fascinates him, as scientist and artist, he manages to convey much of his interest in the human situation to us, too.

Before leaving the fiction of C. P. Snow there is just one further point to make. It is a small one but none the less illustrative of Snow's thoroughness in tackling the job of establishing character. Pamela Hansford Johnson (Lady Snow) is reported in *Books* (March/April 1962) as having given this bit of advice in a National Book League lecture, to any young writer in her audience :

> Whatever characters come into your book, even the most minor . . . write a character sketch of them in a little notebook. Write something about their background. . . . You won't use it, but it does stop those minor characters from being absolutely pure cardboard. The difference it makes is enormous.

Pamela Hansford Johnson told her listeners that this tip had been passed on to her by her husband. Anyone who has studied C. P. Snow's way of going about the business of fiction writing will recognize how characteristic it is of him.

A man must choose. . . . Men of affairs must make decisions about this question and that man. Sir Hector Rose in *Homecomings* had to make up his mind quickly about Lufkin and George Passant; and with his higher Civil Service approach he very nearly regards an 'error of judgment' as worse than incest. What shall be done about project X? Who will head the Committee, Y or Z? Much of Snow's dynamic comes from asking these questions in one setting or another; a Cambridge college, an atomic research station, the private suite of an industrialist. A close student of three highly advanced societies — the British, American and Russian — and of the 'establishments' that operate them, Snow again and again comes back to this question of choice. He leads off in his Godkin Lectures at Harvard, in 1960 (see *Science and Government*, 1961) with a re-statement of just this problem :

> One of the most bizarre features of any industrial society in

30

our time is that the cardinal choices have to be made by a handful of men: in secret: and, at least in legal form, by men who cannot have a first-hand knowledge of what those choices depend upon or what their results may be.

Science and Government does two jobs. First, it outlines the several choices that faced English and American scientists and administrators in 1940-1, and later in 1945, with regard to research into the making and use of the atom bomb. We all know that the decisions then taken have in the post-war period brought a new dimension into world affairs. Those decisions were to mark the beginning of a new era in world history as surely as the dimming of the lights in Europe in 1914 ended an age of relative security.

Second, Snow's book leads on to discussion of ' closed politics ', as he calls it. Open politics we know about or flatter ourselves we know about since they are always being discussed at different levels: press, platform, TV., pubs. Secret, or ' closed politics ', are another matter altogether, although of course there is nothing new about secrecy in high places. It is as old as human affairs; it has always been practised, and in much the same way. What *is* new is that a man like Snow takes us inside the committee and board rooms, and gives us a vivid, minute-by-minute description of what actually happens. He has formulated his concept of ' closed politics ' from first-hand experience.

Snow maintains that ' closed politics ' can be divided into three kinds: (*a*) committee politics (tennis clubs, factory dramatic groups etc.); (*b*) hierarchical politics (organisations with a chain of command: the armed services, a bureaucracy, a large industry) and (*c*) court politics (power exercised through one man who possesses concentrated authority, as seen in its purest form in the Lindemann-Churchill relationship). Those of us who have never even eaves-dropped on the games that are played in high places must feel indebted to Snow for putting us in the picture. Some of what he has to reveal ought indeed to give any sensitive person a shiver down his spine. Is it re-assuring, for instance, to learn that in ' closed politics ' personalities and personal relations ' carry a weight of responsibility which is out of proportion greater than any they carry in open politics '? All the same we must not blind ourselves to the cold facts of power which we should do well to understand as fully as possible, even though we outsiders may be faintly shocked by the way men of power are willing to consider large numbers of human beings as expendible. These men will sleep in comfortable beds even though millions starve, or thousands are killed and injured and made homeless, for example, by concentrated bombing. Their secret choice has meant that some Japanese still suffer and die from the effects of atomic radiation. Each of us can choose whether to apply to these men the adjectives ' callous ' or ' realistic '.

The earlier part of *Science and Government* gives an account of the struggle between two attitudes towards the proper conduct of the last war: radar versus strategic bombing, radar being championed by Tizard and concentrated bombing by Lindemann (Lord Cherwell). Lindemann, having the ear of Churchill, won the fight, even though his statistics on the likely German mortality figures were disputed at the time and later proved utterly wrong. Snow, in giving the details of the Lindemann-Tizard clash, might well have been writing one of his novels. Kathleen Nott commented shrewdly in *Encounter* (February 1962): ' His treatises can read like novels — and sometimes his novels like blueprints '.

One of the conclusions Snow draws from the events he outlines and analyses in *Science and Government* is that there ought to be a broader scientific foundation for social and administrative decisions. Scientists, he asserts, have ' the gift of foresight' (the reference is to Snorri, the old Icelandic saga character) and without foresight our society will eventually crumble. Snow has a case, an excellent one, and yet perhaps he sometimes overstates it. Does a knowledge of the Second Law of Thermodynamics in itself guarantee ' foresight ' or even a minimum of human decency? Obviously not, and Snow himself is the first to criticise scientists who are simply dishonest (Howard in *The Affair*) or blind to the significance of the

32

individual in society. Whatever one's own reservations about putting our future almost exclusively into the hands of the scientists, Snow has — and not least in *Science and Government* — presented the viewpoint of the responsible scientist-administrator with vigour and clarity.

C. P. Snow has for years contributed occasional articles to the serious national press both in England and, increasingly, in the United States. One has the feeling that sometimes he decides to send up a ' balloon ' before making up his mind whether the time is ripe for a fuller consideration of a given topic. The journals in which he chooses to appear are those with a wide circulation among thoughtful people : *The Sunday Times, The Observer, New Statesman, The New York Times.*

He again took up the theme of the ' new men ' in a *Sunday Times* article ' New Men for a New Era ' (August 24, 1958). Here he touches on the problem of what kind of men are to see us through the years ahead. He grumblingly concedes that the new men must necessarily be ' disciplined, unexhibitionistic, capable of subduing their egos '. Smooth and conformist, perhaps, but Snow believes : ' These are just the people fit to cope with the dangers ahead : they are a profound response to a situation where we can't be anarchic and survive '. It largely depends on one's particular age-group as to whether one is willing to accept the necessity for this somewhat colourless organisation man. But those of us who would prefer to see even a managerial being possessed of a little gaiety and humour and even a touch of unpredictability, must realise that in all highly industrialised communities rooms at the top are being claimed more and more by the sand-papered, industrious men with the virtues of their obvious limitation. If one may lift a phrase or two from *Homecomings* it may be said that these men combine ' zest for detail and executive precision ' but are lacking in ' long-term imagination '.

A more heartening subject was explored in ' The Moral Grandeur of Einstein ' (*New Statesman,* March 26, 1960), based on *Albert Einstein, Philosopher-Scientist,* a symposium edited by Paul Arthur Schilpp. Here we are told something of the conflict between those eminent men who differed in their approach to the ultimate description of the physical world. Einstein put his faith in a unified field theory; others, notable among them being Niels Bohr, argued the case for the statistical quantum theory. Snow deplores his inability to communicate these arguments to a lay public that knows little or nothing of physics but in speaking of Einstein he gives us a useful and striking analogy: ' It is rather as though Picasso, in 1920, at the height of his powers, had announced that representational painting alone could be made to contain the visual truth, and had proceeded single-handed to practise it for thirty years.' Images like that do help to convey at least a *human impression* of the physicists' war of ideas.

Snow's description of his visit to Einstein, on Long Island, on a hot day in June 1937 brings the man to life. They ate open sandwiches of *wurst,* cheese and cucumber, and drank nothing but soda-water. Einstein told Snow that creative work whether in science or the arts is almost never done when a man is unhappy and could think of only one exception in science. ' To understand the world,' said the great man with finality, ' one must not be worrying about oneself.'

C. P. Snow must have little time free in which to worry about himself; but it is clear that he ' worries ' (or at least *thinks*) a good deal about the political and human situation. A lengthy article of his called ' The Great Delusions ' (*Observer,* December 31, 1961) makes that fact clear. In it he concerns himself with the question: will the United States repeat the mistakes made by Britain? Among the bubbles he pricks are these: that American engineers (or British) are the best in the world; that in the eyes of some wishful-thinkers the first great Soviet space-flight did not take place; that the coloured races are inferior in all ways to the white. He puts forward his viewpoint with a more than usual asperity and insistence, no doubt because he believes that the basic conditions of life cannot improve either in Britain or the United States until the educated population in both countries is prepared to accept a

34

number of unpalatable truths. These are rammed home with vigour.

In the past five years or so the rise of C. P. Snow to prominence not only as a creative writer but as a ' wise man of the tribe ' has brought forth a spate of critical comment. Sides have formed for and against. Professional critics have tended either to give his books their warm approval or to declare war *à l'outrance*. Dr. F. R. Leavis has declared war on Snow in no uncertain terms and his vicious attack in the Richmond Lecture at Downing College, Cambridge (the text of which was reprinted in *The Spectator,* March 9, 1962), has made literary history. We would need to go a long way back into the English past to find an attack informed by so much concentrated venom.

' Snow is in fact portentously ignorant,' we are told, before Dr. Leavis proceeds to sneer : ' I have no doubt that *he* can define a machine-tool and state the second law of Thermo-dynamics.' Dr. Leavis then makes the amazing statement : ' He is intellectually as undistinguished as it is possible to be.' When a critic makes assertions of this kind we begin to suspect his motives. Here is another of Dr. Leavis's inelegantly expressed revelations : ' Snow is, of course, a — no, I can't say that; he isn't : Snow thinks of himself as a novelist '. He remarks a little later, in reference to Snow's novels : ' I am trying to remember where I heard (can I have dreamed it?) that they are composed for him by an electronic brain called Charlie, into which the instructions are fed in the form of the chapter-headings.' Now surely that is just typical of the vulgar abuse that might pass for wit in a four-ale bar. Dr. Leavis might at least have attempted to use a rapier rather than a cosh.

And so the attack goes on : ' He knows nothing of history ' and ' The intellectual nullity, apparent in his way with the term " culture " is only emphasised for us when, coming to his other culture, that of the scientist, he makes, as himself, a scientist, his odd show of concern for a " high conceptual level ".' The reader must judge for himself whether sentences like that add anything at all to the serious discussion of C. P. Snow's views on literature, history and the place of science in contemporary society. On the rare occasions when Dr. Leavis deviates into lucid prose his vulgar over-statement makes one doubt whether he had anything of importance to convey to his listeners at Cambridge. He takes great pains to weaken his own case.

Lest the present writer should be accused of so strong a partisanship for Snow's writing that he is unwilling to make any concessions at all to Dr. Leavis, it might be well to quote, first of all, the reactions of two creative writers of distinction from among those who came to Snow's defence. (See *The Spectator*, March 16, 1962). Dame Edith Sitwell wrote:

> I read with an entire lack of interest, but some surprise, Dr. F. R. Leavis's non-stop and malevolent attack on Sir Charles Snow in your last issue.
>
> I read to the end of this attack solely because I could not make out what it was all about, or why Dr. Leavis wrote it.
>
> Is it possible that Sir Charles may have offended Dr. Leavis by the fact of his great fame, or by the fact that he — Sir Charles — can write English?
>
> Only this can explain such a silly exhibition.

William Gerhardi had this to say of Dr. Leavis:

> You may consider that Shakespeare got Leavis's number when he said of him: ' This is some fellow, who, having been praised for bluntness, doth affect a saucy roughness. . . . He, an honest mind and plain, he must speak truth. . . . These kind of knaves I know, which in this plainness harbour more craft and more corrupter ends than twenty silly-duckling observants that stretch their duties nicely '. That is why he is in the dock. He is charged on three counts: insincerity, incapacity and envy. You must, there-fore, consider not his works, but his probable intentions. You have to read between the lines.
>
> The operative word upon which he relies to justify the gangster warfare he has inaugurated as a new form of literary criticism, in the attempt to assassinate the reputation of an eminent contem-porary, is: duty. Commando means employed to a noble, if un-specified, end. That is his defence. But read between the lines, his message is: ' Down with Snow and up with Leavis! ' That is all it is.

Dr. Leavis singled out Snow's dialogue for special attack. It is interesting, therefore, to have the view of Ronald Millar, the man responsible for the highly successful stage version of *The Masters,* first presented at the Strand Theatre :

> Lashing out wildly at Snow's dialogue, Leavis says : ' To imagine it spoken is impossible.' But to imagine it spoken is unnecessary. He can, in fact, *hear* it spoken at one of the London theatres. True, Snow wrote the book on which the play is based, not the play itself. But I think I should know the balance of the dialogue between dramatist and novelist. If I put it at roughly fifty-fifty, I am no doubt, like Leavis, doing C. P. Snow a gross injustice.

Before leaving the sad spectacle of this angry, intolerant don, who likes to talk almost as if he and he alone had invented George Eliot and D. H. Lawrence, one must refer to the most ridiculous aspect of his attack. That is, while admitting to being a non-scientist himself, Dr. Leavis calls Snow a *bad* scientist. Professor J. D. Bernal, a scientist of the greatest distinction, has taken up this point in *The Spectator,* March 23, 1962. Reasonable people, whether scientists or not, will be prepared to listen to Professor Bernal's view :

> Dr. Leavis claims to refute the very concept of the two cultures by the simple device of reducing to nullity this world of science of which he prides himself on being totally ignorant. What is insufferable is for this ignoramus to sneer at Snow for being no scientist.
>
> I worked with Snow at Cambridge in the most exciting year of 1932 when the neutron was discovered and *Scrutiny* founded. He was a brilliant physical chemist whose work on photo-chemistry in the solid state could easily have opened up for him a new field of research. His abandonment of active work in science at this point was a most deliberate and voluntary choice which he explains freely enough in *The Search.* Snow was more interested in scientists as people, and in their effect on the world they lived in. When he came to write novels he maintained and extended his interest in science, with which he always remained sensitively in contact. What evidently fascinated him most was the use to which science was put in government and industry. And he was not content to write about it. He lived and worked in it. He held no sinecures. His work in the Civil Service Commission, particularly during the

war on the National Register, showed his real ability for getting the most out of people by understanding them and letting them have their heads. If the Germans had been able to find a man of the same calibre to make as good use of their scientists, the victory would have been a far nearer thing than it was.

More moderate and perhaps more highly informed critics than Dr. Leavis have turned their attention to the work and thought of C. P. Snow: and those readers who are sufficiently interested may look up the somewhat technical ' Two Cultures ' controversy in the 1959-60 files of *Encounter*. There they will find critical comment on a level worth respect. Snow replied to his *Encounter* (and other) critics in a long article in the February 1960 issue of that journal. Just as Dr. Leavis quoted D. H. Lawrence against Snow, so did G. H. Bantock (*The Listener*, September 17, 1959). In his defence against that particular line of attack, Snow points out how careful we must be in accepting too literally the truth of the Lawrentian phrase about putting our trust in ' the instinctive heart '. Did not Adolf Hitler do precisely that? More central to the argument, perhaps, is Snow's assertion that the artistic and intellectual moment always seems more permanent than it really is in fact.

Hence he recalls how Ibsen wrote in 1882 to George Brandes: ' I hold that that man is in the right who is most closely in league with the future.' Snow affirms his belief that this view may again be held at the end of the present century by the ' Russian, American, English masters ' just as it was held by Tolstoy and Chekov. He believes that it depends on whether we can, in our time, bring about a fusion of the two cultures. Certainly, if we can, a great deal of the credit will be due to the pioneer work of C. P. Snow himself.

William Cooper's *C. P. Snow* (Writers and Their Work, No. 115: 1959) is an excellent summing-up. Leaving aside the ideological content, adverse critics have in general concentrated their fire on Snow's style. Bernard Bergonzi, in a well-reasoned essay in the *Twentieth Century* (March 1960) attacks Mr. Cooper's defence of Snow's prose style and pronounces it ' functionally disabling ', whatever that means. Mr. Bergonzi takes strong exception to William Cooper's analysis of it and in particular to his claim that 'Snow's style . . . has been developed firstly to give *absolute conviction* on the plane of immediate fact. . . .' Mr. Bergonzi believes, on the contrary, that ' a weakness of Lewis Eliot's role as narrator and central intelligence in *Strangers and Brothers* is that he is, much of the time, too close to "the plane of immediate fact"'. Critics differ, but the present writer feels that William Cooper is in the right by a quite appreciable margin in the concluding sentences of his pamphlet. These may be considered not merely in relation to C. P. Snow's prose style but to his entire achievement as a creative writer.

> It has a compelling tone which arises not only, or even mainly, from knowledge, but from the author's total involvement in what he is doing. To read it is to believe it. The fact that Snow has such a wide experience and understanding of life in England naturally gives what he writes a peculiar authority; his style, simple, unaffected and moving, is such as to make what he writes immediately recognizable as plain truth.

Each of us, according to his experience and range of interest, must in the end judge for himself. The best any critic can do is to make an interim assessment as honestly as he can and with a fitting sense of humility. Nobody is infallible, not even Dr. F. R. Leavis. The reader is therefore invited to turn directly to C. P. Snow's work and decide for himself whether he does not find running through it the voice of a 'human brother'.

BIBLIOGRAPHY

by Bernard Stone

Note

In the ' STRANGERS AND BROTHERS ' sequence of novels, the suggested reading order is as follows : —

1. STRANGERS AND BROTHERS :   (1925-1933)

2. THE CONSCIENCE OF THE RICH :   (1927-1936)

3. TIME OF HOPE :   (1914-1933)

4. THE LIGHT AND THE DARK :   (1935-1943)

5. THE MASTERS :   (1937)

6. THE NEW MEN :   (1939-1946)

7. HOMECOMINGS :   (1938-1948)

8. THE AFFAIR :   (1953-1954)

The Uniform Edition of the above sequence of novels has not been listed in the Bibliography, but it is now published by Macmillan & Co. Each is bound in blue cloth, with a dust-jacket designed by SIDNEY NOLAN.

A new novel in this sequence will be published by Macmillan & Co., in the Spring, 1963, under the title — ' THE CORRIDORS OF POWER '.

They will also publish, in one volume, the play by Ronald Millar, adapted from the novel ' THE AFFAIR ', together with his forthcoming adaptation of ' THE NEW MEN '.

A French translation of ' THE AFFAIR ' is also scheduled for publication, by Editions Robert Laffont, Paris.

Harvard University Press, Cambridge, Mass., U.S.A. will be publishing, during the Summer, 1962, ' APPENDIX TO SCIENCE AND GOVERNMENT '.

Two of the novels — ' THE LIGHT AND THE DARK '

and ' DEATH UNDER SAIL ' — have recently appeared in Polish translation.

During the latter part of 1962, Russian translations of ' THE AFFAIR ' and ' TIME OF HOPE ' will be published. Several articles have already appeared in Russia, entitled : —

    (*a*) The Cosmos and Man's Progress (at the time of Gargarin's space-trip);

    (*b*) Some notes on Humanism;

    (*c*) The Scientific Revolution and Literature.

I wish to record my thanks to the following for their enthusiastic assistance : —

Miss Freda M. Haddy, Secretary to Sir Charles Snow;

Miss Margit Rostock, Librarian, Deutsches Kulturinstitut, London;

Mr. I. Kaye, Librarian, The Royal Society of London;

The Staff of Kensington Central Library.

Officials of the British Museum Library.

and also acknowledge the co-operation of : —

British Broadcasting Corporation, London;

Cambridge University Press, London;

Deutsche Verlags-Anstalt, Stuttgart;

Doubleday & Co. Inc., New York;

M. D. Elevitch, Esq., Editor — FIRST PERSON, New York;

Evans Plays, London;

Faber & Faber, Ltd., London;

Victor Gollancz, Ltd., London;

Granada TV., Manchester;

Hamish Hamilton Ltd., London (for Harper and Brothers, New York);

Harvard University Press, Cambridge, Mass.;

William Heinemann Ltd., London;

Editions Robert Laffont, Paris;

Lyric Opera House, London;

Macmillan & Co. Ltd., London;

The Macmillan Company, New York;

The Macmillan Company of Canada, Ltd., Toronto;

The Mid-Century Book Society, Inc., New York;
National Book League, London;
P. A. Norstedt & Soner, Stockholm;
Oxford University Press, London;
Penguin Books Ltd., Middlesex;
Polish Cultural Institute, London.
Rutgers University Press, New Brunswick, N.J.;
Charles Scribner's Sons, Ltd., London;
St. Martin's Press, Inc., New York;
Strand Theatre, London;
World Books, The Reprint Society Ltd., London;
Paul Zsolnay Verlag, Vienna.

B.S.

The 'Turret' Bookshop.
London.
1962.

1 : B O O K S :

B.1. DEATH UNDER SAIL:
A : First Novel : A Detective Story : London : Heinemann : 1932 :
B : Detective Library : (2/6d.) London : Heinemann : 1938 :
C : Revised and Reprinted : London : Heinemann : 1959 :

B.2. NEW LIVES FOR OLD:
Published Anonymously : (with Title only, on spine and title-page). Black cloth : pp-399 : crown 8vo : London : Gollancz : 1933 :

B.3. THE SEARCH:
A : London : Gollancz : 1934 :
B : Indianapolis : New York : Bobbs-Merrill Co : 1935 :
C : Revised Edition with Preface : London : Macmillan : 1958 :
D : New York : Scribner : 1958 :

B.4. RICHARD ALDINGTON:
An Appreciation : with Bibliography : Pamphlet : pp-26 : frontis : issued free of charge : London : Heinemann : 1938 :

B.5. STRANGERS AND BROTHERS:
A : London : Faber : 1940 :
B : London : Macmillan : 1951 :

44

C: New York: Scribner:
1960:

D: New York: The Mid-
Century Book Society, Inc:
1960:

E: Penguin Paper Covered
Edition: 1962:

B.6. THE LIGHT
AND THE DARK:

A: London: Faber: 1947:

B: New York: The Macmillan
Company: 1948:

C: London: Macmillan: 1951:

D: New York: Scribner:
1961:
Translations:

E: DIE LICHTEN UND DIE
DUNKLEN GEWALTEN:
tr: Dr. Walter Puchwein:
Wien: Zsolnay: 1948:

F: LA LUMIERE ET LES
TENEBRES: tr: Renee
Villoteau: Paris: Laffont:
1952:

B.7. TIME OF HOPE:

A: London: Faber: 1949:

B: New York: The Macmillan
Company: 1950:

C: London: Macmillan: 1951:
(The Faber Sheets, includ-
ing the Title-Page with the
Faber imprint, were used
for this Edition):

D: New York: Scribner:
1961:

E: New York: Harper &
Brothers: Torchbook Series:

45

Paper Covered Edition:
1961:
F: Penguin Paper Covered
Edition: 1962:
Translations:
G: JAHRE DER HOFF-
NUNG: tr: Edmund Th.
Kauer: Wien: Zsolnay:
1951:
H: LE TEMPS DE L'ESPOIR:
tr: Renee Villoteau: Paris:
Laffont: 1953:
I: ZEIT DER HOFFNUNG:
tr: Grete Felten: Stuttgart:
Deutsche Verlags-Anstalt:
1960:

B.8. THE MASTERS:
A: London: Macmillan: 1951:
B: New York: The Macmillan
Company: 1951:
C: Penguin Paper Covered
Edition: 1956:
D: New York: Doubleday:
Pocket Book: Anchor
Series: 1959:
E: New York: Scribner: 1960:
Translations:
F: DIE LEHRER: tr: George.
Goyert: Munchen: Desch:
1952:
G: REKTORSVALET: tr:
Jane Lundblad: Stockholm:
Norstedt: 1954:

B.9. THE NEW MEN:
A: London: Macmillan: 1954:
Awarded James Tait Black
Memorial Prize:
B: New York: Scribner: 1954:

C : Penguin Paper Covered
Edition : 1959 :
D : New York : Paper Covered
Edition : Scribner Library :
1961 :
Translations :
E : DE NYA MANNEN :
tr : Jane Lundblad :
Stockholm : Norstedt :
1956 :

B.10. HOMECOMINGS : A : London : Macmillan : 1956:
B : New York : Scribner : 1956:
Translations :
C : HEMKOMSTER :
tr : Jane Lundblad :
Stockholm : Norstedt :
1960 :

B.11. THE CONSCIENCE
OF THE RICH : A : London : Macmillan : 1958:
B : New York : Scribner : 1958:
C : New York : Paper Covered
Edition : Scribner Library :
1960 :
D : Penguin Paper Covered
Edition : 1961 :
Translations :
E : DAS GEWISSEN DER
REICHEN :
tr : Rolf Michaelis :
Stuttgart : Deutsche
Verlags-Anstalt : 1961 :

B.12. THE TWO
CULTURES AND
THE SCIENTIFIC
REVOLUTION : The Rede Lecture : 1959 :
Wrappers : pp-52 : with

47

notes: London: Cambridge University Press: 1959:

B.13. THE AFFAIR:

A: London: Macmillan: 1960:
B: New York: Scribner: 1960:
C: New York: Book of the Month Club, Inc: Choice No. 409: 1960:
D: London: The Reprint Society Limited: World Books: June, 1961:
E: Penguin Paper Covered Edition: 1962:

B.14. SCIENCE AND GOVERNMENT:

Harvard University Godkin Lectures on the Essentials of Free Government and the Duties of the Citizen, 1960:
A: Cambridge, Massachusetts: Harvard University Press: 1961:
B: London: Oxford University Press: 1961:
Translations:
C: POLITIK HINTER VERSCHLOSSENEN TUREN-WISSENS-CHAFT UND STAATSFUHRUNG: tr: Grete & K. E. Felten: Stuttgart: Deutsche Verlags-Anstalt: 1962:

B.15. MAGNANIMITY:

Rectorial Address by C. P. SNOW: (Sir Charles Percy Snow, Kt., C.B.E., LL.D., D.Litt.)

48

Delivered before the University
of St. Andrews: 13th April,
1962:
Wrappers: pp-23: frontis:
Published by the University of
St. Andrews Students Repre-
sentative Council — Macmillan
& Co. Ltd: 1962:
(the reprint in May 1962 does
not have the Macmillan imprint)

2 : CONTRIBUTIONS TO BOOKS :

CB.1. SATURDAY
BOOK No. 8
1948 :

Edited by Leonard Russell:
London: Hutchinson:
contains: ' THE
MATHEMATICIAN ON
CRICKET ':

CB.2. SATURDAY
BOOK No. 9
1949 :

Edited by Leonard Russell:
London: Hutchinson:
contains: ' WISDOM OF
NIELS BOHR ':

CB.3. ESSAYS AND
STUDIES 1961 :

Being Volume 14 of the
new series of Essays and
Studies collected for The
English Association: by
Derek Hudson:
London: John Murray:
1961:

contains:
' ITALO SVEVO — Fore-
runner of Cooper and
Amis ':

CB.4.   THE OPEN
      FORM: Edited by Alfred Kazin:
                          New York: Harcourt
                          Brace: 1961: contains:
                          ' THE TWO CULTURES '
                          (excerpt):

CB.5.   THE FATE OF
      MAN :   Edited by Clarence Crane:
                          New York: Braziller:
                          1961: contains:
                          ' THE LITERATI AND
                          THE SCIENTISTS ':

CB.6.   WINTER'S
      TALES 7:   A : Stories from Modern Russia:
                             Edited and with an intro-
                             duction by C. P. Snow and
                             Pamela Hansford Johnson:
                             London: Macmillan: 1961:
                       B : STORIES FROM
                             MODERN RUSSIA:
                           New York: St. Martin's
                           Press: 1962:

A SERIES OF ONE-ACT PLAYS:
by Pamela Hansford Johnson and C. P. Snow:
London: Evans Brothers Limited: 1951:

CB.7.   THE SUPPER DANCE:

CB.8.   FAMILY PARTY:

CB.9.   SPARE THE ROD:

CB.10. TO MURDER MRS. MORTIMER:

CB.11. THE PIGEON WITH THE SILVER FOOT:

CB.12. HER BEST FOOT FORWARD:

3 : CONTRIBUTIONS TO SCIENTIFIC JOURNALS

1. PROCEEDINGS OF THE ROYAL SOCIETY OF LONDON :

SERIES ' A ' :

'INFRA-RED INVESTIGATIONS OF MOLECULAR STRUCTURE':

Volume 124, p.442 (1929): PART I. 'APPARATUS AND TECHNIQUE': by C. P. Snow (Keddey Fletcher-Warr Student) and A. M. Taylor (Ramsey Memorial Research Fellow):

Volume 124, p.453 (1929): PART II. 'THE MOLECULE OF NITRIC OXIDE': by C. P. Snow, F. I. G. Rawlins, and E. K. Rideal.

Volume 125, p.462 (1929): PART III. 'THE MOLECULE OF CARBON MONOXIDE': by C. P. Snow and E. K. Rideal.

Volume 126, p.355 (1930): PART IV. 'THE OVERTONE OF NITRIC OXIDE': by C. P. Snow and E. K. Rideal.

Volume 128, p.294 (1930): PART V. 'THE SIMPLEST KIND OF POLYATOMIC MOLECULE': by C. P. Snow (Laboratory of Physical Chemistry, Cambridge):

SERIES ' A ' :

Volume 127, p.271 (1930): 'THE OPTICAL ROTATORY POWER OF QUARTZ ON EITHER SIDE OF AN INFRA-RED ABSORPTION BAND': by T. M.

Lowry, F.R.S., and C. P. Snow.

Volume 149, p.434 (1935): 'ELECTRONIC SPECTRA OF POLYATOMIC MOLECULES': —
1. ' SATURATED ALDEHYDES ';
2. ' ACROLEIN ', by E. Eastwood and C. P. Snow.

SERIES ' B ':

Volume 115, p.261 (1934): ' PHYSICO-CHEMICAL STUDIES OF COMPLEX ORGANIC MOLECULES ': Part I: ' MONO-CHROMATIC IRRADIATION ', by F. P. Bowden and C. P. Snow.

2. DISCOVERY: Published by The Cambridge University Press:
As Editor 1938/40 contributions included:

NEW SERIES :

Vol. 1, No. 7. Oct/1938.	' SCIENCE IN A MODERN WORLD ':
Vol. 1, No. 9. Dec/1938.	Editorial comment—' SCIENCE AND CONSCIENCE ' — on a letter from Mr. Richard Aldington, contained in this issue.
Vol. 2, No. 13. Apl/1939.	' THE FIRST EXCITEMENT THAT KNOWLEDGE GIVES ' — also Editorial comment on letter.
Vol. 2, No. 14. May/1939.	' SCIENCE AND AIR WAR-FARE ':
Vol. 2, No. 15. Jne/1939.	' RACE, NATIONS, CLASS: LESSONS OF GENETICS ':
Vol. 2, No. 16. Jly/1939.	' A NEW ATTEMPT TO EXPLAIN MODERN PHYSICS ':
Vol. 2, No. 18. Spt/1939.	' A NEW MEANS OF DESTRUCTION ':
Vol. 2, No. 19. Oct/1939.	' THE FATE OF HOMO SAPIENS ':

Vol. 2, No. 20. Nov/1939.	' AGAINST DESTRUCTIVE-NESS ': and Book Review by:
Vol. 2, No. 21. Dec/1939.	'THE TRUTH OF GENETICS': (A review of ' YOU AND HEREDITY ', by Amram Scheinfeld):
Vol. 2, No. 22. Jan/1940.	' SKETCHES OF TIME ':
Vol. 2, No. 23. Feb/1940.	' SCIENTISTS AND WAR DISCOVERIES ':
Vol. 3, No. 24. Mch/1940.	(The last issue in this series 'THE END OF DISCOVERY' :

4 : CONTRIBUTIONS TO PERIODICALS :

CP.1.	NATURE:	March 8, 1930: ' COLOURS OF INORGANIC SALTS ': by C. P. Snow and Francis I. G. Rawlins.
CP.2.	NATURE:	June 16, 1934: ' ABSORP-TION SPECTRA OF ALDE-HYDES ': by C. P. Snow and E. Eastwood.
CP.3.	NATURE:	February 2, 1935: ' SOURCES OF ERROR IN ABSORPTION SPECTROSCOPY ': by C. P. Snow and E. Eastwood.
CP.4.	SPECTATOR:	June 12, 1936: ' ENJOYMENT OF SCIENCE ':
CP.5.	SPECTATOR:	October 16, 1936: ' FALSE ALARM IN PHYSICS ':
CP.6.	SPECTATOR:	November 20, 1936: ' WHAT WE NEED FROM APPLIED SCIENCE ':

CP.7.	SPECTATOR:	December 4, 1936: 'SUPER-FLUITY OF PARTICLES':
CP.8.	SPECTATOR:	April 16, 1937: 'HUMANITY OF SCIENCE':
CP.9.	SPECTATOR:	October 22, 1937: 'CONTROLLING REPRODUCTION':
CP.10.	SPECTATOR:	January 28, '38: 'BRIGHTEST THINGS IN THE UNIVERSE':
CP.11.	SPECTATOR:	September 22, 1950: 'BOOKS AND WRITERS':
CP.12.	SPECTATOR:	January 19, 1951: 'BOOKS AND WRITERS':
CP.13.	SPECTATOR:	March 12, 1954: 'REFLECTIONS ON MR. DEAN'S REPORT':
CP.14.	POLITICAL QUARTERLY:	October, 1944: 'CAREERS':
CP.15.	NEW STATESMAN:	December 25, 1954: 'WELL ENDOWED':
CP.16.	NEW STATESMAN:	September 6, 1956: 'NEW MINDS FOR THE NEW WORLD':
CP.17.	NEW STATESMAN:	October 6, 1956: 'THE TWO CULTURES':
CP.18.	NEW STATESMAN:	March 2, 1957: 'LONDON DIARY':
CP.19.	NEW STATESMAN:	July 27, 1957: Book review by:

CP.20. NEW
STATESMAN : September 6, 1958 : ' WHICH
SIDE OF THE ATLANTIC :
THE WRITER'S CHOICE ' :

CP.21. NEW
STATESMAN : March 26, 1960 : Book Review
by :

CP.22. NEW
STATESMAN : August 11, 1961 : ' MIASMA,
DARKNESS & TORPIDITY ' :

CP.23. MADEMOISELLE: February, 1958 : ' CHANGING
NATURE OF LOVE ' :

CP.24. HOLIDAY : April, 1958 : ' MEN OF FIS-
SION ' :

CP.25. NEW REPUBLIC: August 18, 1958 : ' HABIT OF
TRUTH ' :

CP.26. NEW REPUBLIC: October 27, 1958 : ' ATOMIC
PIONEERS ' :

CP.27. NATION : September 13, 1958 : ' FUTURE
OF MAN ' :

CP.28. ATLANTIC
MONTHLY : November, 1958 : ' AGE OF
RUTHERFORD ' :

CP.29. TIME AND
TIDE : March 14, 1959 : Book Review
by :

CP.30. SCIENCE : August 21, 1959 : ' TWO
CULTURES ' : (excerpt from
SEARCH).

CP.31. SCIENCE : December 23, 1960 : ' BRING
ON THE SCIENTISTS ' : (ex-
cerpt from address).

CP.32. SCIENCE: January 27, 1961: 'MORAL UN-NEUTRALITY OF SCIENCE': (address).

CP.33. SATURDAY
EVENING POST September 12, 1959: 'CON-FLICT OF CULTURES':

CP.34. MEANJIN: October, 1959: 'AN OBJECT OF LOVE':

CP.35. THE LONDON
MAGAZINE: October, 1959: A Letter:

CP.36. ENCOUNTER: No. 74: November, 1959: Book Review by:

CP.37. ENCOUNTER: No. 77: February, 1960: The 'Two Cultures' — Controversy, Afterthoughts:

CP.38. ENCOUNTER: No. 101: February, 1962: 'CONVERSATION PIECE': Malcolm Muggeridge — C. P. Snow: (extract from Transcript of TV. programme).

CP.39. WRITING IN
AMERICA: Edited by John Fischer and Robert B. Silvers: Rutgers University Press: New Brunswick; New Jersey: 1960: (First British Publication — November 1960.) Based on the 1959 Harper's Magazine Supplement: contains 'WHICH SIDE OF THE ATLANTIC':

CP.40. NEWSWEEK: April 11, 1960: 'ADDING UP EINSTEIN':

CP.41. TWO CITIES
REVIEW: No. 4: May 15, 1960: **An**
·   Interview:

CP.42. LIBRARY
JOURNAL: July, 1960: ' TWO CULTURES
                        AND THE SCIENTIFIC
                        REVOLUTION ':
                        (excerpt from address).

CP.43. TIME: December 12, 1960: ' BRING
                        ON THE SCIENTISTS ': (ex-
                        cerpt from address).

CP.44. LIFE: February 3, 1961: 'WHETHER
                        WE LIVE OR DIE ':

CP.45. SCIENCE
DIGEST: March, 1961: ' MORAL UN-
                        NEUTRALITY OF SCIENCE '
                        (condensation of address).

CP.46. EVERGREEN
REVIEW: Vol. 5. No. 17: March-April,
                        1961: From — THE MORAL
                        UN-NEUTRALITY OF
                        SCIENCE: An excerpt from an
                        address before the American
                        Association for the Advancement
                        of Science on December 27,
                        1960, reprinted from *The New
                        York Times*:

CP.47. COMMENTARY: October, 1961: ' WESTERN
                        VALUES AND TOTAL WAR':

CP.48. LOOK: December 19, '61: ' QUARTER
                        CENTURY: ITS GREAT DE-
                        LUSIONS ':

CP.49. KENYON
REVIEW: Winter, 1961: ' SCIENCE,

POLITICS AND THE
NOVELIST ' :

CP.50.   PARTISAN
          REVIEW :   No. 1 : Winter, 1962 : Contri-
bution to Symposium : ' THE
COLD WAR AND THE
WEST ' :

5 : A SELECTION OF CONTRIBUTIONS TO NEWSPAPERS :

The Sunday Times :
    August 24/1958; December 31/1961; April 22/1962;
    December 28/1962.

The Times Literary Supplement :
    August 15/1958.

The Observer :
    July 13/1958; December 31/1961.

New York Times :
    January 30/1958.

6 : DRAMATISATIONS AND BROADCASTS :

1. ' VIEW OVER THE PARK ' :
    A Play — First performance at the LYRIC Opera
    House, Hammersmith : August 29, 1950.

2. ' THE AFFAIR ' :
    A Play — Adaptation of the Novel by Ronald Millar.
    First performance at the STRAND Theatre, Aldwich :
    September 21, 1961.

3. ' THE MASTERS ' :
    Dramatised for Radio by E. J. King Bull : Broadcast

on The Home Service of the British Broadcasting
Corporation: August 8, 1958.

4. 'MYTH, REALITY AND FICTION':
Frank Kermode introduced recorded conversations
with Iris Murdoch, Graham Greene, Angus Wilson,
Ivy Compton-Burnett, C. P. SNOW, John Wain
and Muriel Spark: Broadcast in The Third Programme of the B.B.C. — March 29, 1962.

5. 'A RETURN TO CAMBRIDGE':
C. P. Snow, Novelist and Scientist, looks again at the
University where he was both student and don:
transmitted by B.B.C. Television: September 15,
1959. (Repeated on April 13, 1960.)

6. 'APPOINTMENT WITH C. P. SNOW':
Interview: Malcolm Muggeridge — C. P. Snow:
Transmitted by Granada Television — August 18,
1961.

7 : SOME CRITICAL STUDIES OF C. P. SNOW :

1. C. P. SNOW, by William Cooper: (Writers and their
Work No. 115.) Published for The British Council
and the National Book League: Longmans, Green
& Co.: Portrait frontispiece.

2. ESSAYS AND STUDIES 1950: Being Volume Three
of the new series of Essays and Studies collected
for The English Association, by G. Rostrevor
Hamilton: London: John Murray: 1950: contains:
THREE NOVELISTS AND THE DRAWING OF
CHARACTER (C. P. Snow, Joyce Cary and Ivy
Compton Burnett), by Pamela Hansford Johnson.

3. ESSAYS AND STUDIES 1961: By Derek Hudson (see
CB.2)—contains: TECHNIQUE AND CULTURE.
Three Cambridge Portraits, by S. Gorley Putt.

4. READING A NOVEL, by Walter Allen: London, Phoenix House: Revised Edition 1956 — Contains Essay on 'THE MASTERS':

5. THE NOVEL 1950-1955, by Walter Allen. (Bibliographical Series.) Published for The British Council and the National Book League: Longmans, Green & Co., 1955 (and reprint 'THE NOVEL TO-DAY', 1960).

6. A GATHERING OF FUGITIVES: New Essays, by Lionel Trilling: London, Secker & Warburg, 1957— contains: 'THE NOVEL ALIVE OR DEAD' (first appeared in 'THE GRIFFIN', 1955).

7. THE ENGLISH UNIVERSITY NOVEL, by Mortimer R. Proctor: University of California Press: Berkeley and Los Angeles: and Cambridge University Press: 1957 — contains: 'THE CULT OF OXFORD'.

8. COLLEGE ECHOES — Editors: Douglas Findlay, Bruce Tulloch. Published by the St. Andrews Committee, S.R.C.: October, 1961 — contains: 'C. P. Snow', by Alastair MacKenzie (a Literary appreciation).

9. THE PELICAN GUIDE TO ENGLISH LITERATURE: Edited by Boris Ford, 'THE MODERN AGE'. Penguin Books, 1961—contains: 'NOVELISTS OF THREE DECADES': Evelyn Waugh, Graham Green, C. P. Snow: by Graham Martin: and 'THE NOVEL TODAY', by Gilbert Phelps.

10. PUZZLES AND EPIPHANIES: Essays and Reviews 1958-1961, by Frank Kermode: London, Routledge, 1962 — contains: 'BECKETT, SNOW, AND PURE POVERTY' (from ENCOUNTER—No. 82 July, 1960).

11. PARTISAN REVIEW: No. 1. Winter, 1957—contains: Review of 'HOMECOMINGS', by R. W. Flint.

8 : A SELECTION OF PERIODICAL AND NEWSPAPER CRITICISMS AND REVIEWS :

BOOKMAN (LONDON):
August, 1932; December, 1933.

NATION:
February 2, 1957; June 25, 1960; January 7, 1961.

SATURDAY REVIEW:
February 22, 1958; July 12, 1958; May 7, 1960; March 4, 1961.

ENCOUNTER:
No. 58.	July, 1958.
No. 63.	December, 1958.
No. 71.	August, 1959.
No. 76.	January, 1960.
No. 82.	July, 1960.
No. 93.	June, 1961.
No. 95.	August, 1961.
No. 100.	January, 1962.
No. 101.	February, 1962.

THE NEW YORKER:
May 10, 1958; December 16, 1961; March 24, 1962.

COMMONWEAL:
October 12, 1956.

CRITIQUE:
Spring-Summer, 1958.

THE HUMANIST:
October, 1958.

THE REPORTER:
February 5, 1959; June 9, 1960.

TIME:
July 6, 1959; May 16, 1960.

TIME AND TIDE:
  June 27, 1959.

SPECTATOR:
  August 7, 1959; March 9, 1962; March 16, 1962;
  March 23, 1962; March 30, 1962.

NEW STATESMAN:
  March 29, 1958; May 29, 1958.

LISTENER:
  September 10, 1959; September 17, 1959.

THE LONDON MAGAZINE:
  November, 1959; January, 1962.

MEANJIN:
  Vol. 6. No. 3 : 1960.

TWENTIETH CENTURY:
  March, 1960; June, 1960; July, 1960.

A REVIEW OF ENGLISH LITERATURE:
  Vol. 1. No. 2. April, 1960: ('The Contemporary
  Novel ').

KENYON REVIEW:
  Fall, 1960.

CAMBRIDGE REVIEW:
  November 7, 1960.

VOGUE:
  March 1, 1961.

LIFE:
  April 7, 1961.

DISCUSSION:
  April 1, 1961.
  Proceedings of the American Academy & National
  Institute of ARTS & LETTERS, and Series No. 12,
  May 24, 1961.

BULLETIN OF THE ATOMIC SCIENTISTS:
October, 1961; February, 1962.

BOOKS: The Journal of the N.B.L.:
March/April, 1962.

TOPIC:
November 25, 1961.

NEWSWEEK:
January 15, 1962; March 5, 1962.

BOOKS AND BOOKMEN:
March, 1962; May, 1962.

THE TIMES LITERARY SUPPLEMENT:
March 28, 1958; May 1, 1959; May 22, 1959;
August 7, 1959; March 4, 1960; September 9, 1960.

THE SUNDAY TIMES:
August 24, 1958; March 4, 1962.

NEW YORK TIMES:
January 4, 1959.

THE TIMES:
April 5, 6, 7, 1961.

JOHN O'LONDONS WEEKLY:
February 4, 1960; May 12, 1960.

DAILY TELEGRAPH:
April 14, 1960; April 14, 1962.

THE GUARDIAN:
March 20, 1962; April 14, 1962.

THE SCOTSMAN:
April 14, 1962.

9 : EPHEMERA :

1. The Sunday Times Publication: 'GREAT BOOKS OF OUR TIME', 1961 (includes 'STRANGERS AND BROTHERS').

2. Sotheby & Co. Catalogue of Sale: December 12, 1961.

3. The Guardian: May 5, 1962. (Miscellany: Michael Frayn.)

4. FIRST PERSON: A new concept in creative publishing. Edited by M. D. Elevitch, Boston, Mass. Volume 1. No. 3: Spring/Summer, 1961 — contains:
   a. J. C. (pen name for Jon Cohen), 'THE TOO CULTURED' (satire pertaining to The Two Cultures and the Scientific Revolution);
   b. Dan Pinck, 'FRIENDS AND SISTERS' (parody of Lewis Eliot novels).

5. 2 Prospectuses issued by the Deutsche Verlags-Anstalt, Stuttgart:
   a. DAS GEWISSEN DER REICHEN — (THE CONSCIENCE OF THE RICH), and ZEIT DER HOFFNUNG — (TIME OF HOPE); 4pp. with extracts from reviews.
   b. ZEIT DER HOFFNUNG: 8pp. with extracts from reviews, criticisms. Photo.